EDGE BOOKS™

DINOSAUR WARS

ALLOSAURUS

★ ★ ★ ★ ★ ★ ★ ★ ★ ★

VS.

BRACHIOSAURUS

★ ★ ★ ★ ★ ★ ★ ★ ★ ★

MIGHT AGAINST HEIGHT

by Michael O'Hearn

Consultant:
Mathew J. Wedel, PhD
Paleontologist and Assistant Professor
Western University of Health Sciences
Pomona, California

CAPSTONE PRESS
a capstone imprint

Edge Books are published by Capstone Press,
151 Good Counsel Drive, P.O. Box 669, Mankato, Minnesota 56002.
www.capstonepress.com

092009
005619WZS10

 Books published by Capstone Press are manufactured with paper
containing at least 10 percent post-consumer waste.

Library of Congress Cataloging-in-Publication Data
O'Hearn, Michael, 1972–
    Allosaurus vs. Brachiosaurus: might against height / by Michael O'Hearn.
    p. cm. — (Edge books. Dinosaur wars)
    Includes bibliographical references and index.
    Summary: "Describes the features of Allosaurus and Brachiosaurus,
and how they may have battled each other in prehistoric times" — Provided
by publisher.
    ISBN 978-1-4296-3935-4 (lib. bdg.)
    1. Allosaurus — Juvenile literature. 2. Brachiosaurus — Juvenile literature.
I. Title. II. Series.
QE862.S3O34 2010
567.912 — dc22   2009028073

Editorial Credits

Aaron Sautter, editor; Kyle Grenz, designer; Marcie Spence, media researcher;
    Nathan Gassman, art director; Laura Manthe, production specialist

Illustrations

Philip Renne and Jon Hughes

Photo Credits

Shutterstock/Leigh Prather, stylized backgrounds
Shutterstock/Steve Cukrov, 18 (top)
Shutterstock/Valery Potapova, parchment backgrounds

TABLE OF
CONTENTS

WELCOME TO DINOSAUR WARS!

Dinosaurs were brutal creatures. They fought each other and ate each other. Usually it was meat-eater versus plant-eater or big versus small. But in Dinosaur Wars, it's a free for all. Plant-eaters attack plant-eaters. Giants fight giants. And small dinosaurs gang up on huge opponents. In Dinosaur Wars, any dinosaur battle is possible!

In this dinosaur war, Allosaurus and Brachiosaurus bash it out. You'll see how Allosaurus hunts dinosaurs much larger than himself. You'll discover how both dinosaurs fought and defended themselves. You'll learn about their very different weapons. Then you'll see them battling head-to-head — and you'll get to watch from a front row seat!

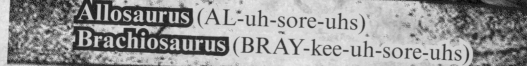

Allosaurus (AL-uh-sore-uhs)
Brachiosaurus (BRAY-kee-uh-sore-uhs)

THE COMBATANTS

ALLOSAURUS VS. BRACHIOSAURUS

Allosaurus might have hunted Brachiosaurus. Both dinosaurs lived in the same parts of the world. They lived in western North America, Portugal, and parts of Africa. Allosaurus **fossils** have been found in Australia too. Both beasts lived from 150 to 145 million years ago. And both became extinct about 144 million years ago.

Brachiosaurus was one of the largest dinosaurs ever. In fact, he was so large that he had to spend most of his time eating. With all that meat on his bones, he would have looked like a delicious meal to a hungry Allosaurus.

While he was alive, Allosaurus was the largest **predator** on earth. But even the fiercest Allosaurus would have a hard time killing the giant Brachiosaurus. He would need some help. Some scientists believe Allosaurus may have hunted in packs. Packs could have helped Allosaurus take down a Brachiosaurus.

While he was alive, Allosaurus was one of the most common dinosaurs on earth. Scientists have found more fossils of Allosaurus than any other large predator.

FIERCE FACT COMMON PREDATORS

fossil — the remains of an animal preserved as rock

predator — an animal that hunts other animals for food

SIZE

Allosaurus was a big, powerful predator. He weighed up to 3.5 tons (3.2 metric tons). He measured about 40 feet (12 meters) long from head to tail and stood about 16 feet (5 meters) tall. That's about as heavy as a full-sized SUV and as long as a school bus. But as big as he was, Allosaurus was much smaller than the enormous Brachiosaurus.

**Brachiosaurus means "arm lizard."
He was given this name because of
his unusually long front legs.**

FIERCE
FACT
NAME

Brachiosaurus measured 85 feet (26 meters) from head to tail. He stood up to 50 feet (15 meters) tall, which is as tall as a large maple tree. His long neck made up about half of his total body length. Because his front legs were longer than his back legs, his neck and body slanted upward. Brachiosaurus was extremely heavy at 50 tons (45 metric tons). He weighed about as much as 10 adult elephants. Brachiosaurus would have a definite size advantage against Allosaurus.

DEFENSES

Allosaurus
Powerful jaws
★ ★ ★

★ ★ ★
Brachiosaurus
Gigantic size

Wherever he went, Allosaurus was the meanest, baddest dinosaur around. Allosaurus didn't have armor or a club on his tail. His snarling mouth full of sharp teeth was the only defense he needed.

Over many years, the "long neck" dinosaurs like Brachiosaurus evolved to huge sizes to protect themselves from predators. However, the meat-eaters adapted by growing larger too.

FIERCE FACT

HUGE SIZES

Brachiosaurus was too big to pick on. His massive size was his main defense. Brachiosaurus likely traveled in **herds** for defense. If one giant dinosaur was too much to take down, then a whole herd of them would really be a challenge.

herd — a group of the same kind of animal

ALLOSAURUS' WEAPONS

Allosaurus
Sharp teeth and claws
★ ★ ★ ★ ★

Allosaurus' mouth was perfectly designed for chomping meat. His jaw was flexible, and his skull was especially strong. Allosaurus had a gaping bite that could fit around the thickest body parts of his **prey**.

FIERCE FACT FOSSILS

Only about three percent of dinosaur fossils belong to meat-eaters.

His mouth held more than 50 teeth, some as long as steak knives. The teeth were shaped like steak knives too. Allosaurus' teeth were flat on the sides but sharp and **serrated** at the front and back. The serrated edges helped his teeth easily slice through flesh.

Allosaurus also had three clawed fingers on each hand. His claws were more than 6 inches (15 centimeters) long. They were curved to a point like an eagle's talons. The claws helped Allosaurus grab onto even the largest dinosaurs. Allosaurus' natural weapons would be an advantage against any opponent.

prey — an animal that is hunted by another animal
serrated — having a jagged edge

BRACHIOSAURUS' WEAPONS

Brachiosaurus was a **herbivore**. He had few weapons to defend himself. His main weapon was his enormous size. He was big enough to stomp on an attacker. Catching an enemy's leg or tail under his huge foot could cause serious damage.

14

herbivore — an animal that eats only plants

Brachiosaurus had five toes on each foot. One toe on each front foot had a hooked claw. Three toes on each back foot also had claws. These claws weren't as long or as nasty as Allosaurus' claws. But they were long enough and sharp enough to be dangerous in a fight.

Brachiosaurus also had a long, heavy tail and neck. Getting hit with either one could knock even a big predator like Allosaurus off his feet.

Brachiosaurus' thigh bone was more than 6 feet (1.8 meters) long.

FIERCE FACT
BONES

ATTACK STYLE

When on the attack, Allosaurus struck early and often. His strong, "S"-shaped neck allowed him to dart his head forward like a snake. His strong jaw helped him tear away strips of flesh from his prey. He would take shallow bites out of his victim until it grew weak from blood loss. Then he could finish his meal.

Not all fossils are bones. Fossils can also be traces of dinosaur activity, such as footprints preserved in rock.

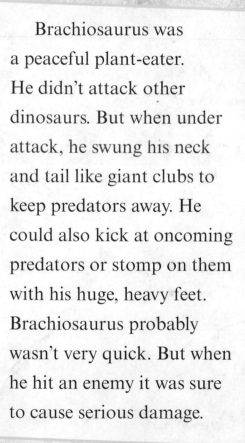

Brachiosaurus was a peaceful plant-eater. He didn't attack other dinosaurs. But when under attack, he swung his neck and tail like giant clubs to keep predators away. He could also kick at oncoming predators or stomp on them with his huge, heavy feet. Brachiosaurus probably wasn't very quick. But when he hit an enemy it was sure to cause serious damage.

GET READY TO RUMBLE!

When the earth shakes under your feet, you'll know this battle is on! It's a clash of the meanest and the mightiest, and there's bound to be some pain. In one corner is the frightening and vicious predator — Allosaurus! He's the meanest meat-eater of his time, and he likes a good fight. In the other corner is his brawny opponent — Brachiosaurus! He isn't looking for a fight, but he's big enough to take out his enemies. This fight is bound to be one for the ages!

ALLOSAURUS

SIZE ★ ★ ★ ✓ ★ ★ ★ ★ ★

DEFENSES ★ ★ ★

WEAPONS ★ ★ ★ ★ ★ ★ ★

ATTACK STYLE ★ ★ ★ ★ ★ ★ ★ ★

BRACHIOSAURUS

You've got a front row seat. So grab your favorite snack and drink, turn the page, and get ready to enjoy the battle!

ONE LAST THING...

These two dinosaurs might have battled in real life. But this fight is made up. No one has ever seen these two mighty beasts go head-to-head. There's no way to know how it would have happened. Still, if you like a good dinosaur smackdown, this one should be totally amazing!

PAIN

Deep, round footprints crisscross a lakeside clearing. The leafy treetops nearby are cropped short, chewed down by a herd of hungry dinosaurs. Several tall heads poke above the trees.

In the clearing, a lone Brachiosaurus reaches his long neck down to sip some cool water. Suddenly, he stops. He hears footsteps. He jerks his head up and cranes his neck to peer into the woods.

Suddenly, a knife-toothed Allosaurus steps out of the woods. He stands about as tall as Brachiosaurus' legs. He stares hungrily at the meaty herbivore.

FIERCE FACT

PACK HUNTERS

Some fossil sites of plant-eating dinosaurs also contain fossils from several different Allosauruses. Some scientists believe these sites prove that Allosaurus hunted in packs.

Then a second, larger Allosaurus steps out of the woods. The first Allosaurus snarls at the newcomer. The larger predator roars and curls his clawed fingers. The first Allosaurus growls and turns his attention back to Brachiosaurus.

Suddenly, all three dinosaurs charge! The two predators run toward Brachiosaurus, who barrels straight ahead. The three beasts crash at the center of the clearing. The impact sends the two meat-eaters flying like bowling pins.

Brachiosaurus keeps running until he reaches the edge of the clearing. The woods are too thick for his giant body. He stops and turns around. His enemies have climbed to their feet and are facing him once more. The Allosauruses open their deadly mouths wide and roar. This battle is about to get nasty!

Brachiosaurus ate the leaves of gingko trees. Many smaller herbivores ate ferns as well as other plants.

FIERCE FACT

FOOD

Brachiosaurus runs. The two attackers chase after him. The ground shakes as Brachiosaurus' feet pound the dirt.

The two meat-eaters come up behind him, one at each hip. They snap at his body, slicing their knifelike teeth into his flesh. Using their strong necks, they tear chunks of flesh from his side. Blood oozes from the wounds.

Brachiosaurus wails. He stops and whips his tail at his attackers. He lands a blow on the smaller Allosaurus. It tumbles backward and skids across the ground. The larger Allosaurus strikes again and catches Brachiosaurus on the tail. Again, Brachiosaurus wails.

Brachiosaurus starts to run. But the larger Allosaurus heads him off. He snaps at the herbivore's meaty front leg. Brachiosaurus kicks at his enemy with his clawed foot. The Allosaurus screeches and backs away. A deep gash runs down his back leg.

Brachiosaurus turns away from the predator and rumbles back toward the lake. He finds the smaller Allosaurus standing in front of him. The smaller foe charges, but Brachiosaurus is ready. He swings his long, thick neck and clobbers the attacker, who tumbles to the ground again.

Brachiosaurus thunders across the clearing. The larger Allosaurus races after his prey. Brachiosaurus whips his long tail at the approaching predator. But the Allosaurus ducks under the blow. Then he digs his long, sharp claws into Brachiosaurus' flesh.

While gripping the massive prey, the large Allosaurus snaps down on his victim's back. He rips out more big chunks of flesh. Brachiosaurus howls in pain.

The name Allosaurus means "different lizard."

FIERCE FACT
NAME

Brachiosaurus begins to feel weak. He starts to panic. He thrashes his head and tail at the creature latched onto his back. He wails, bucks, and shakes.

Brachiosaurus steps into the lake with his back foot. He tries to pull himself forward. But the large Allosaurus, still clamped on, bites again. Brachiosaurus jerks backward and loses his balance. He topples sideways and plunges into the lake. He lands on top of his enemy. The larger Allosaurus is crushed beneath his prey's massive weight.

The lake water reaches halfway up Brachiosaurus' body. He is stuck in the thick mud at the bottom of the lake. Weakened by the attack, Brachiosaurus can't climb out. The water turns red where he lies.

At the edge of the lake, the smaller Allosaurus hungrily eyes the fallen Brachiosaurus. He lets out a triumphant screech. He'll eat well today!

GLOSSARY

evolve (ee-VAHLV) — when something develops over a long time with gradual changes

extinct (ik-STINGKT) — no longer living; an extinct animal is one whose kind has died out completely.

fossil (FAH-suhl) — the remains or traces of plants and animals that are preserved as rock

herbivore (HUR-buh-vor) — an animal that eats only plants

herd (HURD) — a group of the same kind of animal

predator (PRED-uh-tur) — an animal that hunts other animals for food

prey (PRAY) — an animal hunted by another animal for food

serrated (SER-ay-tid) — having a jagged edge that helps with cutting, such as a saw blade

READ MORE

Bacchin, Matteo. *The Hunting Pack: Allosaurus*. Dinosaurs. New York: Abbeville Press, 2010.

Dixon, Dougal. *World of Dinosaurs and Other Prehistoric Life*. Hauppauge, N.Y.: Barrons, 2008.

Long, John. *Dinosaurs*. New York: Simon & Schuster Books for Young Readers, 2007.

INTERNET SITES

FactHound offers a safe, fun way to find Internet sites related to this book. All of the sites on FactHound have been researched by our staff.

Here's all you do:

Visit *www.facthound.com*

FactHound will fetch the best sites for you!

INDEX